915.2 Gagne
We visit Japan

YOUR LAND
AND
MY LAND
ASIA

We Visit

JAPAN

Tammy

Gagne

Mitchell Lane

PUBLISHERS
P.O. Box 196
Hockessin, Delaware 19707

YOUR LAND
AND
MY LAND
ASIA

Cambodia
China
India
Indonesia
Japan
Malaysia
North Korea
The Philippines
Singapore
South Korea

YOUR LAND
AND
MY LAND
ASIA

We Visit

JAPAN

Asia

Printing   1   2   3   4   5   6   7   8   9

Library of Congress Cataloging-in-Publication Data
Gagne, Tammy.
 We visit Japan / by Tammy Gagne.
       pages cm. — (Your land and my land: Asia)
 Includes bibliographical references and index.
 ISBN 978-1-61228-479-8 (library bound)
 1. Japan—Juvenile literature. I. Title.
 DS806.G18 2013
 952—dc23
                                                    2013033973
eBook ISBN: 9781612285344

PUBLISHER'S NOTE: This story is based on the author's extensive research, which she believes to be accurate. Documentation of this research is on page 61.

   The internet sites referenced herein were active as of the publication date. Due to the fleeting nature of some websites, we cannot guarantee they will all be active when you are reading this book.

PBP

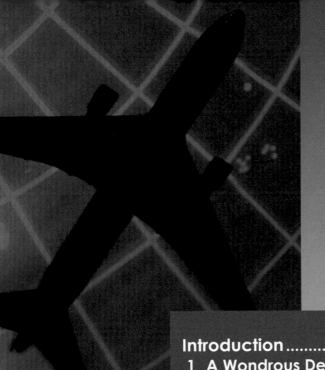

Contents

Introduction

Japan lies just to the east of the continent of Asia. Called an archipelago, the country is made up of more than 6,800 mountainous islands, though only about 400 are inhabited. Scientists think that at one time both Japan and the Asian mainland were part of a bigger land mass called Pangaea (Greek for *all land*). Over the course of millions of years, Pangaea broke apart due to weaknesses in the earth's crust. The various pieces became the continents and the many islands as they exist today. This widely held belief is known as the plate tectonics theory.

Among the evidence supporting this theory are the many fossils that archaeologists have found in Japan. Ancient skeletons of large animals like elephants and rhinoceroses have been unearthed throughout the country. Since Japan lies well over a hundred miles from the nearest point of the Asian mainland, these animals could not get to the island by swimming. They must have walked across land to get there.

It is believed that people have lived on the Japanese islands for more than 35,000 years. It is only just over a thousand years, however, that Japanese history has been recorded.

A special test train nicknamed Dr. Yellow runs on a Japanese high-speed line to ensure the safety of the track. Mt. Fuji, one of Japan's most famous landmarks, is in the background.

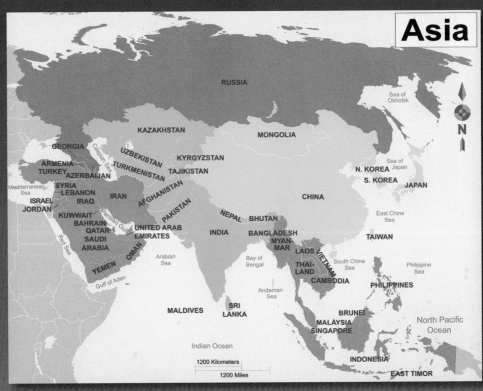

Asia

RUSSIA

Sea of Okhotsk

KAZAKHSTAN

MONGOLIA

GEORGIA
ARMENIA
TURKEY
AZERBAIJAN
Caspian Sea
UZBEKISTAN
TURKMENISTAN
KYRGYZSTAN
TAJIKISTAN
N. KOREA
S. KOREA
JAPAN
Sea of Japan

Mediterranean Sea
SYRIA
LEBANON
ISRAEL
JORDAN
IRAQ
IRAN
AFGHANISTAN
PAKISTAN
CHINA
East China Sea

Persian Gulf
KUWWAIT
BAHRAIN
QATAR
UNITED ARAB
EMIRATES
NEPAL
BHUTAN
INDIA
BANGLADESH
MYAN-
MAR
TAIWAN

SAUDI
ARABIA
OMAN
Red Sea
Arabian Sea
Bay of Bengal
LAOS
THAI-
LAND
VIETNAM
South China Sea
Philippine Sea

YEMEN
Gulf of Aden
CAMBODIA
PHILIPPINES

Andaman Sea

MALDIVES
SRI
LANKA

BRUNEI
MALAYSIA
SINGAPORE
North Pacific Ocean

Indian Ocean

INDONESIA

EAST TIMOR

1200 Kilometers
1200 Miles

N

Akihabara is a popular tourist destination. Located in Tokyo, this district caters to young visitors. Hundreds of shops line the streets, selling the latest electronic items. Tourists can also find shops specializing in anime, manga, and dozens of other pop culture pastimes. Some people call the neighborhood Electric Town because of its bright flashing lights.

A Wondrous Destination

Japan offers its citizens and tourists one of the most fascinating cultural experiences in the world. Steeped in traditions thousands of years in the making, the country has a deeply compelling history. Evidence of this history can be witnessed from virtually any area within the nation. At the same time, Japan is a major contender in the modern world. The nation is a leader in technology, providing the world with many of the electronic tools that people utilize every day.

Japan seems to offer something for everyone. Some visitors to Japan enjoy taking part in a traditional Japanese tea ceremony in Kyoto in the afternoon. Everything about the ceremony—from the food and the utensils to the paintings on the walls—plays an important role. The spiritual experience of the ceremony is meant to promote harmony, respect, purity, and tranquility. Another visitor may prefer to spend an evening in Akihabara, the district of Tokyo often referred to as Electric Town. Many tourists say that this area's bright flashing lights, arcades called pachinko parlors, and numerous anime shops make a trip to Akihabara feel like a visit to the future.

Although the entire country of Japan is roughly the size of California, most tourists find it impossible to see everything they want to see in a short trip. For tourists who live elsewhere in Asia, a return visit might be an easy solution. For visitors flying to the country from the opposite hemisphere, however, it may be smarter to plan a longer stay.

Kiyomizu-dera, located in Kyoto,
is one of the most-visited
Buddhist temples in Japan.

South Koreans are the largest percentage of Japan's tourists. This could change in the coming years, however, as Japan is trying to lure more Chinese visitors to the country. In 2010, more than one million Chinese travelers visited Japan. The Japan Tourism Agency wants to more than triple this number. One reason is the amount of goods Chinese tourists bought in 2010. In just the first five months of the year, the sale of goods to Chinese visitors increased by 40 percent compared to the previous year.[1]

Japan has much to offer tourists in terms of attractions. Many of the most popular sites for visitors are located in Tokyo, Japan's capital. According to the Japan National Tourist Organization, Tokyo is home to seven of the country's most visited sites. A *shinkansen*, or bullet train, can whisk visitors to attractions in outlying areas.

Lined with skyscrapers, Tokyo's Shinjuku district provides many visitors with their first look at the country. The district is filled with hotels, restaurants, and shopping as well as a large number of nightclubs.

An extremely popular shopping area is the Ginza neighborhood, which abounds with high-end boutiques. While their parents are browsing through Fendi or Gucci products in these boutiques, young people enjoy visiting Shibuya and Harajuku, the city's twin centers of teen culture. Families visiting Tokyo should also visit the city's museums and zoo. Many tourists enjoy seeing the old-style temple district called Asakusa as well.

Visitors who prefer more traditional attractions are often drawn to picturesque cities such as Osaka and Kyoto. Even during a short trip, it is easy to visit both of these cities, which are located only about an hour from each other. The former capital of Japan, Kyoto is filled with temples and Zen meditation gardens. The city is also home to the Osaka Aquarium, one of the most popular attractions of its kind in the country. Those interested in castles can tour Osaka Castle and Himeji Castle. The latter attraction, now a World Heritage Site, was built during the 14th century and has undergone several extensive remodelings since then.

Tokyo Disneyland opened to visitors in 1983. This popular vacation spot, modeled after the Walt Disney resorts in Florida and California, was the first Disney theme park outside the United States. A sister park, called Tokyo DisneySea, opened in 2001.

Tourists have another type of castle to explore in Osaka. Universal Studios opened its first international version of the Wizarding World of Harry Potter in 2014. Visitors to the park take in Hogwarts Castle and enjoy rides such Harry Potter and the Forbidden Journey. The theme park, which has entertained millions at Universal's resort in Orlando, Florida, is likely to be a big hit with Japanese fans as well. Potter-themed toys and other products have also been extremely popular with Japanese fans.

Brad Globe, the consumer products president of Warner Brothers, explains, "This type of immersion is what the fans crave more than buying traditional merchandise. Our strategy is focused on theme parks because it's a different experience. They've read the books and seen the movies, but now they can enter the world."[2]

Japan has plenty of natural attractions as well. One of the most famous is Mount Fuji, the country's tallest peak. Travel writer Ken Belson says, "Mount Fuji, or Fujisan as it's known to the Japanese, is the nation's most recognizable natural landmark, a conical volcano immortalized by artists like Katsushika Hokusai and Utagawa Hiroshige. These days, the mountain, less than two hours from Tokyo, is a playground for rich and poor. Climbing the mountain is on many hikers' bucket lists."[3] Because of its popularity and importance to the Japanese, the mountain is on the UNESCO World Heritage list as a cultural asset.

FYI FACT:

The currency of Japan is called yen. In 2013, about 100 yen equaled one U.S. dollar.

Where in the World

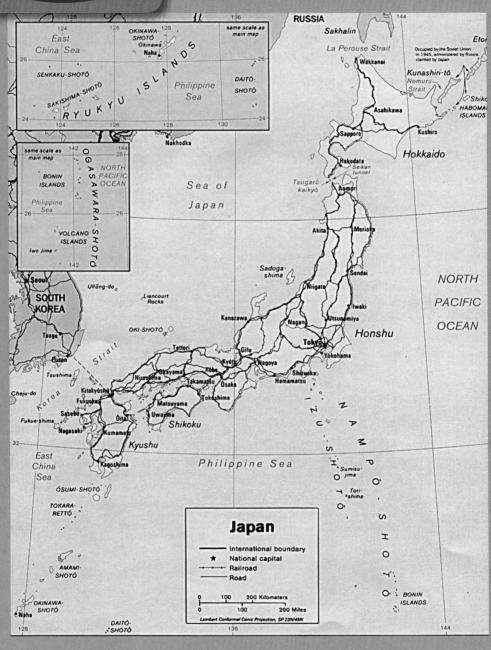

JAPAN FACTS AT A GLANCE

Official Country Name: Japan
Official Language: Japanese
Population: 127,253,075 (July 2013 estimate)
Land Area: 234,825 square miles
(608,194 square kilometers);
slightly smaller than California
Capital: Tokyo
Government: Parliamentary government with a constitutional monarchy
Ethnic Makeup: Japanese 98.5%, Koreans 0.5%, Chinese 0.4%, other 0.6%
Religions: Shintoism 83.9%, Buddhism 71.4%, Christianity 2%, other 7.8% (Note: this total
exceeds 100%, as many people believe in both Shintoism and Buddhism)
Exports: motor vehicles, semiconductors, iron and steel products, auto parts, plastic
materials, power-generating machinery
Imports: petroleum, liquid natural gas, clothing, semiconductors, coal, audio and visual
apparatus
Crops: rice, potatoes, sugar beets, mandarin oranges, cabbage
Average Temperatures:
Tokyo: 84°F (29°C) in summer, 36°F (2°C) in winter
Average Annual Rainfall:
Tokyo: 66.1 inches (167.9 centimeters)
Highest Point: Mount Fuji – 12,388 feet (3,776 meters)
Longest River: Shinano River – 228 miles (367 kilometers)
National Flag: Japan's flag has only two colors. The simple design includes a plain white
background behind a bright red circle which symbolizes the sun. The Japanese people
call the flag "Nisshohki" or "Hinomaru," which means *sun disc*. A legend states that a
Buddhist monk gave a similar flag to the emperor of Japan during the 13th century.
Since that time the flag has changed only slightly, with the most recent modification in
1999 when the disc was moved slightly to the hoist side.
National Sport: sumo wrestling
National Flower: None officially. If asked to name an unofficial national flower, however,
many Japanese would choose either the sakura (cherry blossom) or the chrysanthemum
(long the symbol of the Japanese imperial family).
National Bird: None officially, although the ibis, the crane (often featured in Japanese art)
and the kiji (green pheasant) are all extremely popular birds within the country.
National Tree: Japanese cedar (*Cyrptomeria japonica*)

Source: CIA World Factbook: Japan

近松勘六源行重

給人　禄三百石

浅野家譜代の臣にして誠忠
無二の勇士うり力量つく
ら馬鎗剣ふ熟達す
國家山變法後大石ふ
ミつぶひ京都ふきを
ら仮住ーそのぞ
江戸へ下り
盟約の士と共れ
十辛万苦ーて偽の
虚そろぶひ終り本意を
達せーとぞ

刃隨露劍信士

行年三十四才

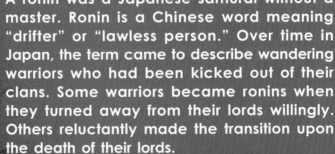

A ronin was a Japanese samurai without a master. Ronin is a Chinese word meaning "drifter" or "lawless person." Over time in Japan, the term came to describe wandering warriors who had been kicked out of their clans. Some warriors became ronins when they turned away from their lords willingly. Others reluctantly made the transition upon the death of their lords.

The History of Japan

The first known inhabitants of Japan came from Siberia to the north and from Korea to the southwest. It is likely that some ancient people also traveled east to Japan from China.

For most of Japanese history, history was relayed orally through stories passed down from one generation to the next. In 712 CE, the *Kojiki* was written.[1] The country's oldest historical record, which is made up of three books, also includes a great deal of mythology. In fact, the history and myths contained in these books are so connected that is hard to tell where one leaves off and the other begins.

The *Kojiki* begins during a period known as *Kamiyo,* or the Age of the Gods. It starts with the Japanese creation myth. According to the story, both heaven and earth were created out of vapor to fill the vast emptiness that came before them. The Three Creating Deities lived in heaven for millions of years before the world below was filled with thousands of gods. When the deities saw that the earth was in chaos, they decided to send a divine couple named Izanagi and Izanami to earth. In turn, the couple created other gods. They are also credited with creating the islands of Japan itself with the tips of their spears.

The earliest rulers of Japan were said to be descendants of Izanago and Izanami and therefore divine. Historians refer to this family as the Yamato line, and the first ruler was Jimmu. According to legend, his reign began in 660 BCE. If one counts all the other rulers mentioned in the *Kojiki,* the fifteenth emperor was Ojin. His reign, which took place in the 4th century CE, marked an important change in the way the Japanese people looked at their rulers. Before this time, Japanese emperors were seen as powerful due to their ability to communicate with the spirit world. Beginning with Ojin, rulers of Japan were admired for their military skills. Ojin's tomb, which is 610 feet (186 meters) long, is one of the largest burial mounds of ancient Japan. It was filled with military instruments. Both the size and the contents show how much the emperor was valued. Ojin's son, Nintoku, was given a far bigger tomb. It measured 1,595 feet (486 meters) in length, making it the world's largest burial structure.[2] Thousands of workers were needed to create such large structures.

Just as impressive as the Yamato family's high status with the Japanese people was its ability to remain the ruling clan of the country for more than 2,000 years. Under Yamato rule, the Japanese people prospered. The Japanese had adopted new agricultural methods from mainland Asia, and new grains were brought to the area as well. Because they were well-fed, Japanese families grew both in terms of numbers and strength. Some more powerful families might have overthrown the Yamato clan if not for the cleverness of the imperial family.

The Yamato clan decided to rank all the Japanese clans from the most powerful to the least. The most powerful ones were moved near the imperial court and named the *omi* and the *muraji*. The Yamato clan made a two-part promise to these families:

The Japanese artist Osai created this work, "Painting of the United States East India Squadron in Tokyo Bay."

First, the Yamato vowed to provide both clans with rice, a food regarded nearly as important to the Japanese people as life itself. Second, the Yamatos promised that all future emperors would select their brides from these two important families.

This agreement assured the *omi* and *muraji* that they would continue to flourish under Yamato rule. It also made them *gaiseki*, or in-laws, of the royal family. Of course, the Yamato also benefitted from the arrangement. It kept the most powerful clans nearby, where the ruling clan could watch them carefully. Also, if other families decided to rebel against the Yamato, the *omi* and the *muraji* were more likely to fight for the Yamato clan than against them.

For centuries Japan did not have much interaction with the rest of the world. From the 17th to the 19th centuries, Japan did a small amount of trade with the Netherlands and China. However, Japan kept its ports closed to the rest of the world. This situation changed when United States naval officer Commodore Matthew Perry led a powerful fleet to Japan in 1853.

The commodore had two main objectives: establishing a peace agreement with Japan's people and opening up trade between the two countries. At first Japanese officials would not even speak with Perry.

This shows steamships from the U.S. Navy entering the Japanese harbor.

But they soon realized that they must consider his requests or face an attack. On March 31, 1854, the two countries signed the Treaty of Kanagawa, which included both peace and trade agreements. Japan created similar agreements with other countries in the years that followed.

Japan maintained a peaceful relationship with the United States until the years leading up to the beginning of World War II. Between 1931 and 1937, Japan had begun attacking China to expand its territory. In an effort to stop Japanese aggression, the U.S. imposed sanctions on Japan. This move would stop trade with Japan and seriously affect its access to oil and other important natural resources.

The battleship USS _Arizona_ was bombed during Japan's attack on Pearl Harbor. This event, which occurred on December 7, 1941, killed 1,177 of the ship's crewmen. It marked the entry of the United States into World War II.

Instead of backing off, Japan attacked American forces at Pearl Harbor, Hawaii on December 7, 1941. At virtually the same time, they assaulted British and Dutch colonies in Southeast Asia. The U.S. responded by declaring war on Japan. For the Japanese, the Pearl Harbor attack would prove to be an example of winning the battle, but losing the war. By June of 1942, the United States had halted Japanese expansion, but the war continued with heavy casualties on both sides. On August 6, 1945, the U.S. dropped an atomic bomb on the city of Hiroshima. This action was followed by a second bomb dropped on Nagasaki three days later. Japan formally surrendered to the United States and its allies on September 2, 1945.

The war years were a time of devastating losses for Japan. But the country proved to be very resilient. The United States occupied Japan from 1945 to 1952 and helped reform the country's political, military, and social systems. The United States also helped Japan begin rebuilding its economy. In just a few decades, Japan became one of the largest economies in the world.

This view of Hiroshima, Japan, shows some of the immense destruction resulting from the atomic bomb that was dropped on August 6, 1945.

白山権現

Shinto shrines can be found throughout Japan.
People who follow Japan's ancient religion go
to these spots to worship. This small Shinto
shrine is called Hakusan Gongen. It is located
at Kita-in Kawagoe, a city about 20 miles
(32 kilometers) northwest of Tokyo.

Japan's first religion was Shintoism. It remains one of the two most common religions in Japan today. Meaning "the way of the gods," Shintoism is different from most other world religions in numerous ways. First, Shintoism does not have a founder. It also doesn't have scriptures, like the Christian Bible does, that its followers can refer to for guidelines. Right and wrong are not spelled out for Shinto followers. No one is expected to be perfect. People are seen as basically good. When people do bad things, the Shinto religion asserts that evil spirits are to blame.

Shinto gods are called *kami*. These entities are believed to take the forms of earthly objects and concepts such as mountains, rain, wind, or even Amaterasu, the sun goddess. When a loved one dies, that person also becomes *kami*, revered by the family members who are left behind.

Purity plays an important part in the Shinto religion. When Izanagi returned from seeing Izanami in the underworld, he bathed to rid himself of *tsumi*. This is the word that the Shinto faith uses for sin or pollution. Shinto followers believe that they can keep evil spirits away through rituals like purification ceremonies, prayer, and offerings to the *kami*.

The biggest difference between *tsumi* and sin is that *tsumi* can even affect a person who makes good choices. In these cases evil spirits are once again believed to be the cause of the problem. Ancient Shinto considered anything related to death or dying as *tsumi*. After touching

In addition to worship, Shinto followers also use shrines as a place for making offerings to the *kami*. The *kami* include gods and goddesses as well as loved ones who have died.

someone who was dying, for instance, people would have to purify themselves through bathing rituals. The warmer the water, the more effective the purification process was believed to be.[1]

Japanese honor *kami* by building shrines for them. Called *jinja*, a shrine is a sacred place where *kami* are believed to live. Each Japanese village has its own shrines that honor the local *kami*, but larger national shrines also exist. Sometimes a shrine is a building, but it doesn't have to be. A shrine can be a hill, a rock, a grove of trees—virtually anything. Likewise, it can extremely large or very small. A large shrine can also be home to many smaller shrines. What matters most is that the shrine is special to a particular *kami*. Many shrines have a strong connection to nature, often blending into the natural landscape.

When visiting a shrine, a person typically claps once to get the attention of the *kami*. The visitor may also scatter rice or salt near the shrine as an act of purification. Japanese people may visit shrines at any time, but the practice is especially common during festivals and before important life events. A couple might go to a shrine to ask the *kami* for good fortune in marriage. They may even choose to hold their wedding ceremony at a shrine for this same purpose.

During the sixth century CE, another important religion came to Japan. The Soga clan had come to Japan from Korea, and they quickly became a high-ranking family in the Yamato court. The Soga clan introduced the Japanese people to Buddhism. This religion began in northern India around the fifth century BCE. By the time it reached Japan, though, it had already been adopted in China, where numerous new elements had been added. At this point in history, China was admired greatly by other Asian nations. Families that had migrated to Japan, as the Soga clan had, saw the spread of Buddhism as evidence of their own influence on Japanese culture.

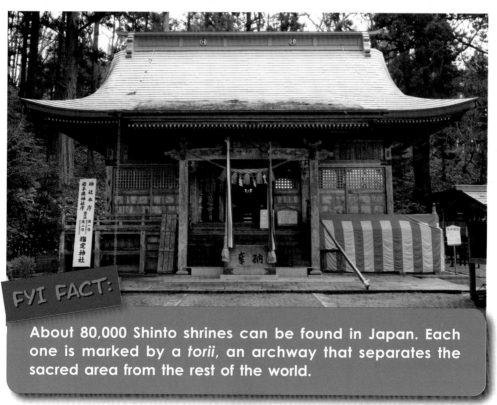

FYI FACT:

About 80,000 Shinto shrines can be found in Japan. Each one is marked by a *torii*, an archway that separates the sacred area from the rest of the world.

Many years have passed since the United States dropped the atomic bomb on Hiroshima, but the people of Japan still mark the anniversary each year with prayers for the victims. On August 6, 2013, the 68th anniversary of the event, Buddhist monks and other guests marked the exact time of the detonation with a moment of silence at 8:15 a.m. in Peace Memorial Park.

Not all Japanese embraced Buddhism, however. Many families saw Buddhism as competition to the Shinto religion. They didn't like the idea of a new faith invading their land. Prince Shotoku of the Soga clan worked hard and long to get the imperial household to accept Buddhism. With more and more high-ranking families coming from Korea and China, this new religion eventually flourished.

Buddhism was founded by the Indian prince Siddhartha Gautama. Better known as the "Enlightened One," or Buddha, he believed that human life was suffering. He also believed that this suffering was caused by desire. Buddhism asserts that by removing selfish desire from human nature, people can achieve enlightenment, or great spiritual knowledge.

Another important part of Buddhism is a belief in reincarnation. Buddha believed that people go through a cycle of birth and rebirth, earning goodwill known as karma by acting selflessly. A person with good karma may be reborn as a person with higher status. Likewise, Buddhists believe that bad actions can follow a person into his or her next life. For example, a person who does bad things in this life might be born as an insect in the next life. To Buddhists, motives matter just as much as actions. A good deed done for selfish purposes is still considered selfish. People who achieve the highest state of enlightenment are said to escape the tortuous cycle of rebirth altogether.

Whereas Shinto followers visit shrines to honor and pray to *kami*, Buddhists go to temples. One of the biggest differences between the two types of altars is that Buddhist temples often contain statues of Buddha. The only statues found at Shinto shrines are of animals, such as foxes or horses. These animals are thought to serve the *kami*. Many Buddhists also have private temples in their homes, complete with smaller statues of the Enlightened One.

Interestingly, many Japanese practice both Shintoism and Buddhism. Although many of the oldest Japanese families were reluctant to accept Buddhism, the two religions are remarkably compatible. Neither belief system contradicts the other in any major way.[2]

Emperor Meiji ruled Japan from 1867 until 1912. This would be a time of many major changes for the country. During his reign, Meiji ordered the end of the feudal land system, started a new school system, and created a cabinet system of government.

The Laws of the Land

For hundreds of years, Japan had no written constitution. Instead, the country's government operated on the *ritsuryo* system, a concept the Japanese had adopted from the Chinese. The first part of the word, *ritsu*, referred to the criminal code. The second part, *ryo*, referred to the administrative and civil codes. Under this system, the government was headed by a grand council of state known as the *dajokan*. This group was in charge of eight ministries, but the real power sat with the emperor who appointed all the officials within the government. Each one was sworn to act as his loyal servant.

The country was divided into provinces, which in turn were divided into districts, villages, and hamlets. One eighth-century document lists 67 provinces with 555 districts, 4,012 villages, and 12,036 hamlets.[1] Each province was led by a governor, but this person was not someone local. Instead these positions were filled by people who came from the capital city of Heijokyo (modern-day Nara). Through this system, the emperor stayed in strict control of the people.

Today the government of Japan works very differently. The constitution of Japan has been in place since 1947. Like the United States, Japan is a democracy. Also like the U.S., the government includes three branches: executive, legislative, and judicial. Although Japan still has an emperor, he is a figurehead with very little political power. At the direction of the Diet, Japan's legislative branch, the emperor appoints the country's prime minister. This person then appoints cabinet members, typically from within the Diet.

Japan's legislative branch of government, the Diet, holds three different types of sessions each year. Ordinary sessions, which begin in January, last 150 days. Extraordinary sessions aren't as structured. They can be called at any time and last different lengths of time. Special sessions are also held under special circumstances—if a prime minister leaves office and has to be replaced, for example.

The Diet is divided into two sections: an upper chamber called the House of the Councillors and a lower chamber called the House of Representatives. All members of the Diet are elected by the citizens of Japan, who must be 20 years old in order to vote.

The biggest difference between Japan's governmental system and that of the U.S. is the exact balance of power among the three branches. In the United States, the executive, legislative, and judicial branches are considered to have equal powers. In Japan, however the legislative branch (the Diet) holds more power than the executive branch (the prime minister and the cabinet) and the judiciary. In this way Japan is more like Great Britain.

All of Japan's laws must be passed by the Diet. This plan is different from the way government works in the United States, where laws can be put into place at the state level as well. In addition to legislation, the Diet is also responsible for approving the national budget, ratifying treaties with other countries or organizations throughout the world, and amending the constitution when deemed necessary.

Although the House of Councillors is considered the upper chamber of the Diet, the House of Representatives has more power when it comes to certain issues. Lawmaking, the selection of the prime minister, the budget, and treaties are all matters in which the lower chamber has more say. As long as two-thirds of the House of Representatives vote for a particular law, they can pass it even if the House of Councillors rejects it.

The House of Representatives consists of 480 members. A person must be at least 25 years old to run for one of these seats. Once a person has been elected, he or she serves a four-term year. Exceptions can occur if the prime minister decides to dissolve the House of Representatives before the end of the terms of its members.

One must be at least 30 years old to serve as one of the 242 members of the House of Councillors. Each chamber includes a standard number of seats to represent each district. The number of remaining seats is based on the population in each district—some districts have more, while others have fewer. Each councillor serves for six years, with half of the members coming up for re-election every

Crown Prince Akihito ascended to the
Japanese throne on January 7, 1989.

three years. Councillors are not removed from office in the event that the cabinet dissolves the House of Representatives.

Like the U.S. Supreme Court, Japan's Supreme Court is the highest court in the nation. Additionally, the country has four types of lower courts. These include eight high courts, 50 district courts—each of which has a family court tied to it—and 438 summary courts. Just as the emperor appoints the prime minister, he also appoints the chief justice of the Supreme Court at the direction of the cabinet. The cabinet appoints the other 14 Supreme Court justices directly.

Each Supreme Court justice must be at least 40 years old. In the United States, members of the Supreme Court are appointed for lifelong positions, although some members do choose to retire. In Japan, however, the voting public has a chance to review each justice every 10 years until the retirement age of 70.

Crown Prince Akihito became the country's 125th emperor when his father, Hirohito, died in 1989. Upon making his first public appearance just a few days later, Akihito remembered that his father "was constantly at one with his people in overcoming the many difficulties in times of turmoil, building today's stability and prosperity and achieving an honored place in international society as a nation of peace....I fervently desire the further development of Japan, peace throughout the world, and a better life for all peoples."[2] Although these words may not sound unusual, the speech was a huge milestone in Japan. No modern emperor before Akihito had ever spoken in public.

As of 2013, the prime minister was Shinzo Abe, who had been elected by the Diet the previous year. Receiving 339 out of the House of Representatives' 480 votes, Abe is said to have won the election by a landslide. He had served in the position of prime minister once before, from 2006 to 2007, but ended up resigning due to health reasons. Between that time and Abe's return, Japan had six different prime ministers, mostly from the Democratic Party of Japan. Abe is a member of the rival Liberal Democratic Party. The word "liberal" can be somewhat misleading here, as Abe and his party are known for having a conservative approach to politics. His top concerns for his country involve strengthening both the economy and diplomacy.

One of Japan's most successful companies is Toyota. Here, a worker checks the paints and bodies of the automaker's Corolla model. This popular model was created in 1968 and is still going strong. Toyota vehicles make up one of the country's biggest exports. They rank as the third best-selling make of automobiles in the United States. They are the world's all-time best-selling passenger car.

Japanese Business and Trade

At his first news conference following his election, Shinzo Abe told the people, "A strong economy is the source of energy for Japan. Without regaining a strong economy, there is no future for Japan.... We must recover a Japan where hardworking people can feel that there is a better tomorrow."[1] The country quickly responded to Abe's message. From November 2012 to April 2013, Japan's stock market went up a remarkable 40 percent.[2] This improvement was good news for a country that had been struggling for more than 20 years.

Abe worked closely with the United States. In April 2013, the two

FYI FACT:

Teaching is among Japan's fastest growing professions. Many people move to Japan from the United States to work as teachers. Instructors fluent in both Japanese and English are in high demand.

Another highly successful Japanese company is the Panasonic Corporation. At this Panasonic plant in Kobe City, workers are assembling the brand's Let's Note laptop computers. The company also manufactures many other types of electric and electronic equipment.

countries made enormous headway in talks over trade. The U.S. made the decision to delay moving quickly on its TransPacific Partnership trade agreement with other countries in the region, thereby allowing Japan to join the conversation.

"Adding Japan will make it very difficult to complete the deal by the end of the year—and is a good excuse for negotiators to delay a bit," said Barbara R. Kotschwar, a research fellow at the Peterson Institute for International Economics. "It is generally recognized that a good deal is more important than a deal that meets a pre-set deadline."[3]

Following the decision to enter talks with the United States, Abe said, "As two of the largest and most advanced economies in the region, Japan and the United States will work together to further enhance economic growth, expand bilateral trade, and strengthen the rule of law."[4]

Japan's biggest exports include automobiles and electronic equipment. The next time you travel by car, take a look around. How many Toyotas, Hondas, and Nissans do you see on the roads of the United States? Your parents may even drive a car from one of these popular automakers, who have created reputations in the United States for selling dependable, economical vehicles. As of 2013, Toyota was the number one automaker in the world.[5] The company also became a trailblazer when it introduced its Prius model, the first widely successful hybrid automobile.

Another well-known Japanese business name in the United States is Mitsubishi, a company known for manufacturing both types of vehicles. The Japanese people, however, know that this enormous

Some of Japan's most extensive terraced rice fields are located in Shodoshima Island, which is also a popular destination for Japanese citizens.

company offers many other goods and services—from stationery products to gas stations.

Look around your home, and you may see the names of other highly successful Japanese businesses. Sony, Panasonic, and Toshiba are among the top names in numerous types of electronics. Like Mitsubishi, these companies also manufacture many items you may not even realize. Even if your computer is a different brand altogether, it is highly likely that it includes parts made by one of these Japanese companies.

In addition to automobiles and electronics, Japan also exports large amounts of iron, steel, and plastic materials. Other than the United States, the country's biggest customers for its exports are China, South Korea, Hong Kong, and Thailand. The United States is the second-largest purchaser, just after China.

Japan imports a large number of goods, especially from China, the United States, and Australia. Among the most common American-made items sold in Japan are agricultural products, chemicals, pharmaceuticals, films and music, commercial aircraft, nonferrous metals, plastics, medical and scientific supplies, and machinery. Japan produces many of its own agricultural products including rice, fruits and vegetables, pork, poultry, dairy products, eggs, and fish.

The country does not export a large number of these food products at this time. Agricultural exports had been on the rise until 2011, when an accident at Tokyo Electric Power Company's Fukushima nuclear power plant instilled great fear over pollution. In the months following the accident, many countries placed restrictions on the importation of agricultural products from Japan, fearing that they could be contaminated by nuclear waste. In the first year after the accident, Japan's agricultural exports dropped by 8.3 percent.[6]

The disaster has also made it necessary for Japan to import more fossil fuels. This change has in turn increased energy costs for the Japanese people. Prime Minister Abe works with the United States to import shale gas to Japan to help with this problem. American industry groups differ in their opinions about the matter. Some fear that an export of this kind could increase energy costs in the United States.

A 9.0-magnitude earthquake struck the northern region of Japan in March of 2011. Following the earthquake, another devastating natural event occurred—a tsunami. This enormous wave, which was created by the earthquake, brought sea water over an embankment and into the city of Miykao. Nearly 19,000 people were killed in the twin tragedies.

Japan's colorful cherry blossoms bring numerous visitors to the country each spring. The flowers come into full bloom each year at the beginning of April. In Japan the blossoms are a symbol of new beginnings. April marks the beginning of the new school year for children, new jobs for many recent graduates, and the start of the new business year for Japanese companies.

A Year Filled with Celebrations

Japan has at least one major festival, holiday, or other type of merriment every month. Some of these celebrations hold deep meaning, while others are more about simply having fun. Japan also shares some of the same holidays with the United States and other countries around the world.

Like the United States, Japan celebrates New Year's Eve on December 31 each year. While most Americans are anxiously looking ahead, though, the Japanese people remain focused on the present day and year. *Omisoka*, the Japanese name for this holiday, provides people with the chance to settle unfinished business. The Japanese see years as being completely separate from one another, so it is very important that any commitments from the current year are honored before the coming year begins. Houses are cleaned, debts are settled, and disagreements are resolved. Once all obligations have been met, *bonekai* (year-forgetting) parties can begin. Along with the current year, the people say goodbye to any troubles or worries they had during the last 12 months.

All of this hard work pays off as soon as *Shogatsu*, the Japanese New Year, arrives on January 1. *Shogatsu* is considered the most important holiday of the year in Japan. Most people spend the first three days of January celebrating this event. It is supposed to be a time filled with happiness and no work or stress of any kind. It is said that the best way to start the celebration is by viewing the first sunrise of the New Year.

On the Japanese lunar calendar, spring begins on either the third or fourth day of February. And with it comes *Setsubun*, the Japanese bean-throwing ceremony. This event dates back to the 13th century, when Japanese people performed some exotic rituals at the start of spring each year. In order to drive away evil spirits, people would burn dried sardine heads and beat drums. They hoped that the strong scent and loud noises would frighten the spirits.

Although *Setsubun* isn't a national holiday, many people still decorate the entrances to their homes with fish heads in keeping with these older traditions. A more modern custom is the scattering of roasted soybeans around one's home to symbolically purify it. When doing this, one is supposed to shout, "Wa soto! Fuku wa uchi!" which means "Get out demon! Come in happiness!" Finally, each person who scatters beans should end the ritual by picking up one bean for every year of his or her age and eating them.[1]

March 3 is known as *Hina-Matsuri*, or Girls' Day. Also known as the Doll Festival, this celebration focuses on the daughters within a family and wishing them health and happiness. In this case the ritual was adopted from China during the latter part of the seventh century and is based on a rather unusual custom. In ancient China it was believed that the sins of a young woman could be transferred from her to a doll. Furthermore, the sins were thought to be removed when the doll was abandoned in a river.

As with *Setsubun*, the Doll Festival has evolved over the centuries. In some areas of Japan, people still float paper dolls down a river on this date each year. Most modern celebrations, though, simply involve displaying dolls throughout the home in celebration of the young girls who live there.

Although the lunar calendar brings spring to Japan in February, the cherry blossoms do not usually appear until April. This is when the *Sakura Matsuri*, or Cherry Blossom Festival, takes place. This breathtaking event draws visitors from all over the world, and is also a special time for Japanese residents who see the blossoms as symbols of human life, transience, and nobleness.

Kodomo-No-Hi, or Children's Day, arrives on May 5 and is one of the most popular national holidays. At one time it was simply known as Boys' Day, a complement of sorts to Hina-Matsuri. In recent years, though, the celebration has included both sexes. In the days and weeks leading up to Kodomo-No-Hi, families place colorful windsocks in the shape of carp outside their homes. Because they are known for swimming upstream against the water's current, carp are a respected Japanese symbol of courage, determination, and strength—all qualities that Japanese parents hope their children will have.

The trees remain in full bloom for only about a week. Depending on the location and weather, this peak viewing season can occur anytime between the beginning of April and the start of May. During this time, many Japanese people hold flower-watching parties called *hanami*.

June and early July is typically a period of wet weather in Japan. This rainy season is called *tsuyu*, which means "plum rain" because it is also the time when this fruit becomes ripe. Many tourists avoid *tsuyu*, but some think Japan's shrines are even more beautiful during the rains. Major attractions in particular are also far less crowded at this time of the year.

If you visit the country during *tsuyu*, you may notice ghost-like dolls hanging in the windows of many houses. Called *teru-teru bozu* dolls, these white decorations made of either fabric or paper are the work of school children. The term means "shine-shine monk," which relates to a song written by Shinpei Nakayama in 1921. "Teru-teru-bozu, teru bozu," the song begins, which means "Do make tomorrow a sunny day." Children sing this song and create these charms in hopes of getting the sun to return soon. The song, based on an old story of a monk who promised to end the rainy season for Japanese farmers, has a rather eerie ending. "But if the clouds are crying [it's raining]," it warns. "Then I shall snip your head off."[2]

Tanabata, or the Star Festival, takes place every year in Japan on the seventh day of the seventh lunar month. Because the Japanese lunar calendar differs somewhat from the regular calendar, some parts of Japan celebrate this festival in July, while others mark the day in August. In both cases, though, the event has come to symbolize love and hope.

The festival is named for two stars, Altair and Vega, which align at this time each year. The stars are symbols for two star-crossed lovers, Hikoboshi and Orihime, who have been separated by the Milky Way. They are said to be able to meet only on this one day of the year. Japanese people have a special custom on this day. Each person writes a wish on a colorful piece of paper, and then hangs it from the branch of a bamboo tree.

In Japan, July and August are also months for remembering family members who have passed on. The exact dates for the three-day Buddhist celebration called *Obon* differ from one region of the country to another, but the purpose is the same. During this religious holiday,

Lanterns hanging in a neighborhood shrine in a small district of Tokyo

Japanese families welcome the spirits of their dead ancestors into their homes. Many prepare altars for the event. They may also spend extra time tending to their loved ones' graves.

Although it sounds like a sorrowful time, *Obon* is actually a celebration of the lives of these lost loved ones. The celebration ends when families launch paper lanterns at the edge of a river or ocean. The candles inside are meant to help guide the souls of the departed family members back to the world of the dead.

On *Undokai*, or Sports Day, Japanese children become athletes—at least for this one day. Students from kindergarten through high school compete in running events, gymnastics, tug-of-war competitions, relay races, and other activities. There are also games unique to Japan, such as *Tama-ire*, a game in which players toss small beanbags into bamboo baskets attached to high poles.

Otsukimi, or the Moon Viewing Festival, occurs in October. Families come together to celebrate the moon and the fall's harvest. Autumn flowers and grasses, which are at their most beautiful during this time, are displayed in homes. Food too is an important part of the celebration. Pumpkin, chestnuts, and white rice dumplings are arranged on family altars as offerings to the moon as a way of showing gratitude for a bountiful harvest.

Certain numbers play an important role in Japanese culture. Odd numbers in particular are regarded lucky. This is seen in *Shichi Go San*, or 7-5-3 Day. This celebration, which occurs each year on November 15, is for boys who are three and five years old, and girls aged three and seven. The children dress up in kimonos and visit Shinto shrines with their families as everyone prays for good health and growth for them. Since turtles and cranes are symbols of longevity in Japan, candies decorated with these animals are given to the children as part of the celebration.

Most Japanese people place school and learning at the top of their priority lists. It isn't unusual for students to take part in athletics or other extracurricular activities, but these pastimes are limited. If a child does play a sport, it is usually the only extracurricular activity in which he or she participates. In the United States, many colleges want to see sports and clubs listed on college applications. In Japan, though, many young people who want to go to college focus entirely on their academic achievements instead.

Language and Learning

Japanese writing looks very different from English writing. In fact, it is different from the way in which most other languages are written. The first thing most Americans and other visitors notice about Japanese writing is that it doesn't use an alphabet the way they do. This quality is part of what makes Japanese writing so interesting, but it is also a large reason why it can be so difficult to learn.

The Japanese writing system is made up of three different scripts: Kanji, Hiragana, and Katakana. The oldest and most complicated of the three is Kanji. Developed in China, this script was brought to Japan during the 5th and 6th centuries CE. Kanji includes thousands of different characters, each representing a different noun, verb, or adjective. Instead of writing a word made up of different letters, the Japanese write a single symbol for a word such as sun, water, or fire. Although this writing method may seem easier than learning how to spell words with an alphabet, it is actually quite difficult. Some symbols are made up of a dozen or more strokes, and each one has to be written just so in order to be correct. Kids start learning these characters in elementary school and continue learning them all the way through high school. A 16-year-old is expected to know at least 1,945 Kanji characters.[1]

Young children—and even foreign adults—who are learning Japanese writing start with Hirigana. This script is also very old. It was created more than 1,000 years ago. Representing different sounds, Hirigana characters are much simpler than Kanji symbols, so they are easier to read and write. This script also includes far fewer characters to memorize. As soon as students know all 46 of them, they can probably read a book written at first-grade level. Hirigana symbols are also used in combination with Kanji symbols to form endings for verbs and adjectives in higher-level writing. This combination helps the writer use different tenses of verbs. For example, Kanji includes a symbol for the verb "to learn." In order to write about what you *learned* (the past tense of *to learn*) yesterday, you would need to use both Kanji and Hirigana.

Like Hirigana, Katakana is made up of 46 different symbols. These characters symbolize foreign words and names. Whereas Hirigana symbols are more rounded (like our cursive writing), Katakana characters are made up of straighter strokes and sharp corners (like our printing). Young people and other students new to Japanese writing usually move on to Katakana after they have mastered Hirigana. Once they know all three, they can read almost anything written in Japanese.

Each area has its own dialect—vocabulary, pronunciation, and usage. Japan has about a dozen different dialects in all. Some are similar to one another; others have very little in common. It is possible for two Japanese-speaking people living in different regions of the country not to be able to understand each other at all.

Technology has helped immensely to close the gaps among the various Japanese dialects. At one time, people living in remote areas of the country had little to no interaction with citizens in other parts of Japan. Radio, television, and the internet have helped introduce what is known as standard Japanese to these regions.

Not only are more people learning standard Japanese, but the standardized language is also making its way into the local dialects. People in different regions are adopting certain words, phrases, and pronunciations and using them along with their individual dialects.

Many children learn their area's dialect at home and standardized Japanese in school, making them fluent in both.

For Japanese children, school begins each year in April. Each school year is divided into three terms. Students have two short breaks, one in spring and another in winter, with a month-long summer vacation. In all, children attend school 240 days each year—60 more than American children.[2]

The Japanese Ministry of Education oversees the curriculum in all public schools. This means that students living in Akita, Kyoto, and Nagasaki (or any other city or town) all receive the same exact education. They learn the same material, they use the same books, and they must pass the same exams. This also differs from the American educational system, in which the individual states decide what to teach and how to teach it.

Nearly all Japanese high schools and universities require students to take entrance exams. Even some private junior high schools and elementary schools have similar tests for admission. These exams create a high level of competition among students. As a means of preparing for the exams of the best high schools and colleges, students may attend special private schools called *juku* in addition to their regular classes. Some students will also spend an additional year or two between high school and college at one of these preparatory schools.

Among the best colleges in Japan are the University of Tokyo and the University of Kyoto. Being accepted into either of these prestigious schools is considered an impressive accomplishment. Japan also has numerous private universities.

One well-known graduate of the University of Tokyo is Takao Doi, a Japanese astronaut who was born in 1958. Doi's work has taken him from the Japanese manned space program to the United States at NASA's Lewis Research Center and the University of Colorado. In 1985, Doi was selected by NASA as an astronaut candidate. He flew aboard STS-87 in 1997 as a mission specialist. During this voyage he became the first Japanese astronaut to perform a spacewalk.[3] A decade later he flew to the International Space Station, where he was the first astronaut to throw a boomerang in outer space.

Born in Kasugai, Japan, Ichiro Suzuki was already a champion in Japanese baseball when he made his way to the United States. He joined the Seattle Mariners in 2001, becoming the second player in U.S. baseball history to win both the MVP and Rookie of the Year awards in a single season. He joined the New York Yankees in 2012.

Sports and Leisure Time

Sports have long been a prized part of Japanese culture. Today both traditional sports and those made popular in the West are enjoyed throughout Japan. Many people enjoy competing in sports. Others prefer to watch from the sidelines.

Japanese children are exposed to sports early in life. Girls often play tennis or volleyball in school, while boys are drawn to baseball or soccer. Both boys and girls learn to swim as part of their physical fitness curriculum at school. Some schools even hold swimming events in the ocean where students swim a mile or farther.

Many kids also take part in sports outside of school. During the summer many Japanese families spend time together swimming, surfing, or scuba diving. In the winter families often go ice skating, skiing, or snowboarding.

By far the most popular spectator sport in Japan today is baseball, which was introduced to the country in about 1870 by an American university professor. The Japanese love baseball so much that many of them are surprised to learn that it is America's national sport as well. Japan's top players compete in Nippon Professional Baseball. It consists of 12 teams divided into two leagues, the Pacific League and the Central League. The winners of each league play in the Japan Series, an event much like America's World Series.

In 1995, Hideo Nomo became the first Japanese player to permanently relocate to the United States to play Major League Baseball. More than 40 others have followed in his footsteps. One is

Akinori Iwamura. Born in Uwajima in 1979, Iwamura was picked in the second round of the NPB draft in 1996 by the Tokyo Yakult Swallows. He became the team's third baseman and also proved to be a capable hitter as he helped Yakult win the 2001 Japan Series.[1] Iwamura moved to second base when the Tampa Bay Rays offered him $4.55 million in 2007. He was traded to the Pittsburgh Pirates in 2010, and also played briefly with the Oakland Athletics that year. Then he returned to Japan to play for the Rakuten Golden Eagles, and in 2012 he re-signed with Yakult.

Ichiro Suzuki, known to many fans as simply Ichiro, is probably the greatest baseball player who made his way from Japan to the United States. Ichiro was born in Kasugai in 1973. He played in Japan's Pacific League for more than a decade before joining the Seattle Mariners in 2001. He won both the Rookie of the Year and Most Valuable Player awards that year, batting .350 and stealing 56 bases. In 2004, he set an all-time record for hits in a single season, with 262, as he won the American League batting championship with a .372 average. He has also won 10 Golden Gloves for his fielding ability and was a 10-time All-Star.[2] He moved to the New York Yankees in 2012. As he approached his 4,000th base hit as a professional, Yahoo! Sports columnist Jeff Passan wrote, "Almost every Japanese baseball fan sees Ichiro with that combination of respect, admiration and reverence. From spirit to skills, Ichiro is the archetypal Japanese baseball player, someone who through hard work, repetition and intelligence maximized his physical skills."[3]

In Japan, baseball is also very popular at the Little League level. School baseball clubs attract considerable attention. Two national high school tournaments are played each year in Japan. One is held in the spring, the other in summer. Just like the professional games, these tournaments are televised nationally, so the entire country can watch the games.

When many people think of Japan, they think of martial arts. Certainly, these sports are still thriving in Japan, as they have for hundreds of years. Aikido, judo, karate, and kendo each offer a

Thierry Fabre from France (in white) defeated Japan's Takamasa Anai to become the 2010 World Judo Champion. The event was held in Tokyo.

different style for students. Aikido is based on the principle that one should not fight force with force. Instead, it focuses on seizing and controlling one's opponent. Because it is gentler than judo and karate, aikido has become especially popular with women and older citizens of Japan.

Judo and karate share many qualities, but they are different from each other, too. Both of these hand-to-hand martial art forms are more combative than aikido. Like aikido, though, judo uses a disarming strategy. In this sport students are taught to use their opponents' force against them. Karate, on the other hand, focuses more on striking the opponent's body.

Kendo is a style of fencing based on the techniques of the Japanese samurai. Students of this martial art form must wear body armor called *bogu*. This protective gear protects the students, as bamboo staffs known

FYI FACT:

Like other Japanese martial arts, kendo awards various different skill levels. Unlike the others, though, a skill of a kendo student cannot be determined from the color of a belt.

as *shinai* are used to strike the opponent's head, chest, and hands during matches.

Baseball may be Japan's favorite modern sport, but sumo wrestling is the country's favorite ancient pastime. Professional sumos may not look like athletes, but they follow a very strict training schedule and focus all their energy on gaining as much weight and building as much muscle as they can. A sumo match consists of two wrestlers who have a simple goal: push the other wrestler down or out of the ring. The first one to do either of these is named the winner.

One sumo wrestler named "winner" many times is Ozeki Kaio. In 2011, Kaio enjoyed his record-setting 1,046th win in the sport.[4] Kaio retired shortly thereafter due to numerous injuries that had troubled him, but he remains one of the most popular sumo in modern Japanese history. Interestingly, Kaio had never planned to become a Sumo wrestler. He had mentioned that he wanted to watch a sumo match as an adolescent, but he now says he wasn't serious at the time. "It was just a little joke," he explains. "People around me gave me a lot of advice, then, I decided. In fact, it was set up for me... Funny, the things you don't like sometimes inspire you by just happening."[5]

When Kaio speaks about his retirement, it's easy to see that he doesn't regret that choice he made so long ago. "I see it [the news about my retirement] on television and it's then that I think it's for real. I'm glad I chose to be in the sumo world and I've met a lot of different people and experienced things I would not have been able to in a different line of work."[6] He points out that he owes his success to more than just his own hard work. "I fought hard to move up the rankings and was able to keep going so long because of the support I've had."[7]

In addition to playing and watching sports, Japanese families also enjoy less-physical leisure activities. Among the most popular ways to spend free time are eating at restaurants and visiting theme parks. Families with kids often plan trips during school vacations to Tokyo Disneyland and Universal Studios Japan in Osaka.

Many families who prefer staying home enjoy playing board games. Similar to chess, *Shogi* is popular with both kids and adults in Japan.

Another popular strategy game is Japan is *Go*. Diehard *Go* fans may even assert that it—rather than baseball or sumo—is the true national sport of the country.

Another popular Japanese pastime is listening to music. One of the country's most beloved singers is a woman named Utada Hikaru. Known in the United States simply as Utada, she released her first album in 1998 when she was just 15 years old. Called *First Love*, it became the best selling album in Asian music history. It sold more than seven and a half million copies in Japan alone. She has recorded three of Japan's top 10 best-selling albums of all time.

Japanese Onigiri

Many Japanese kids eat onigiri for lunch, as snacks, and even on picnics. This rice ball is easy to make and can be tailored to match your personal taste.

Ingredients:
1 package of white rice
1 large can of precooked tuna, salmon, or shrimp (for filling)
Mayonnaise to taste
Seaweed

Instructions:
Prepare the following recipe with adult supervision:
1. Cook rice according to the directions on the package.
2. Once the rice is fully cooked, let it sit for about 20 minutes. This step allows the rice to cool and also helps make it as sticky as possible.
3. While the rice is sitting, mix your fish or shrimp with a spoonful of mayonnaise.
4. Once the rice is cooled, form a small amount into a ball that will fit in your hand.
5. Press a tiny crater into one side of the ball, without pushing all the way to the other side.
6. Spoon a small amount of the filling into this crater.
7. Add a bit more rice to cover the filling and close your hand to mold into a ball once again.
8. Wrap the ball with seaweed.
Refrigerate any leftovers and be sure to eat them within 24 hours.

Japanese Nengajo

Many Americans send out greeting cards every Christmas. Japanese also enjoy sending cards to one another, but they perform this custom as a way of celebrating the New Year. Many Japanese children enjoy making their own New Year's postcards called *nengajo*. Perhaps you would enjoy designing your own *nengajo* cards at the start of the New Year. You only need a few supplies and a Zodiac animal chart.

Materials
- Blank postcards. You can find them at most post offices and office supply stores. You can also make your own by cutting plain white cardstock. Using a paper trimmer or scissors, cut the cardstock into pieces measuring either 4 by 6 inches (10 x 15 centimeters) or 5 by 7 inches (13 x 18 centimeters).
- Zodiac animal chart
- Markers, colored pencils, and/or crayons
- Mailing addresses of family members and friends
- Postcard stamps

Instructions
1. Find the zodiac animal that represents the incoming year.
2. Draw the animal on the front postcard along with a greeting, such as "Happy New Year!" You can be as creative as you like, making the animal look realistic or cartoon-like. You might even add stickers or other embellishments that you can find at the craft supply store.
3. To give your postcards a real Japanese look, check your local library for a book on Japanese writing and include some of those symbols.
4. Finally, address your postcards and put stamps on them before mailing them.

Dates BCE

35,000–30,000 The first known settlers of Japan travel to the island from Siberia and Korea.

Dates CE

712 The *Kojiki* is written.

1853 U.S. Navy Commodore Matthew Perry leads a voyage to Japan to open trade between the two countries.

1894–1895 Japan defeats China in the Sino-Japanese War; China gives up Taiwan to Japan and allows Japan to trade in China.

1904–1905 Japan demonstrates military and naval superiority over Russia in the Russo-Japanese War.

1910 Japan annexes Korea.

1914 Japan joins World War I on the side of Britain and its allies.

1919 The Treaty of Versailles ending World War I gives Japan many German territories in the Pacific, which become military bases before and during World War II.

1923 More than 140,000 people are killed in an earthquake in Tokyo, one of the worst natural disasters in world history.

1926 Hirohito becomes emperor of Japan.

1931 Japan invades Manchuria.

1936 Japan signs an anti-communist agreement with Nazi Germany.

1937 Japan goes to war with China.

1939 World War II breaks out in Europe.

1941 Japan attacks the U.S. naval base at Pearl Harbor, Hawaii; the U.S. declares war on Japan the next day.

1942 Japan occupies the Philippines, Dutch East Indies, Burma, and Malaya; the U.S. Navy wins a decisive victory over Japan at the Battle of Midway.

1945 U.S. planes drop atomic bombs on Hiroshima and Nagasaki; Emperor Hirohito surrenders.

1947 Japan adopts a new constitution, which creates a parliamentary system of government.

1951 Japan signs a peace treaty with the United States and other nations.

1952 Japan regains its independence; the U.S. holds onto several Japanese islands, including Okinawa, for military use.

1956 Japan joins the United Nations.

1964 Tokyo is the site of the Olympic Games, the first time that an Asian nation has hosted the Olympics.

1972 The United States returns Okinawa to Japan, but maintains military bases there.

1982	Japanese car manufacturer Honda opens its first plant in the United States.
1989	Emperor Hirohito dies and is succeeded by his son Akihito.
1995	A major earthquake strikes near Kobe, killing more than 6,000 people.
1997	Japan's economy enters a severe recession.
2002	Prime Minister Junichiro Koizumi becomes the first Japanese leader to visit North Korea.
2004	Japan sends non-combat soldiers to Iraq, the country's first deployment in a combat zone since World War II; they leave two years later.
2006	Shinzo Abe succeeds Koizumi as prime minister.
2007	Abe resigns. He is replaced by Yasuo Fukuda.
2011	Another major earthquake hits Japan and the resulting tsunami devastates the country; the Fukushima nuclear plant is damaged, causing a radiation leak.
2012	Shinzo Abe becomes prime minister again.
2014	Diplomatic ties between Japan and China sink to new lows as claims over history, resurgent nationalism and disputed territory fuel public resentment toward the country.

CHAPTER NOTES

Chapter 1: A Wondrous Destination

1. Mariko Sanchanta and Atsuko Fukase, "Japan Welcomes Chinese Tourists." *The Wall Street Journal Asia*, June 30, 2010.
2. Ben Fritz, "Potter Magic to be Tested Soon in Japan." *Los Angeles Times*, May 10, 2012.
3. Ken Belson, "Mount Fuji, So Popular It Hurts." *New York Times*, August 13, 2013. http://travel.nytimes.com/2013/08/18/travel/mount-fuji-so-popular-it-hurts.html?hpw

Chapter 2: The History of Japan

1. Shimane Prefecture, What is the Kojiki? http://www.japanesemythology.jp/kojiki/
2. Japan: The Official Guide, Tomb of Emperor Nintoku. https://www.jnto.go.jp/eng/location/spot/ruins/nintokutennoryo.html

Chapter 3: Japanese Religions

1. BBC Religion: Purity in Shinto. http://www.bbc.co.uk/religion/religions/shinto/beliefs/purity.shtml
2. United Religions Initiative, Shintoism. http://www.uri.org/kids/other_shin.htm

Chapter 4: The Laws of the Land

1. Japanese Reference, Nara Period. http://www.jref.com/japan/history/nara_period.shtml
2. Michael Berger, "Akihito's First Speech as Emperor." *San Francisco Chronicle*, January 10, 1989.

Chapter 5: Japanese Business and Trade

1. "Shinzo Abe returns as Japan PM." *Indian Express*, December 27, 2012.
2. "Appraising Abenomics: Business in Japan." *The Economist*, April 6, 2013.
3. Tim Devaney, "U.S. Welcomes Latecomer Japan to Trans-Pacific Trade Talks." *Washington Times*, April 12, 2013.
4. Ibid.
5. Micheline Maynard, "Toyota Pushes Past GM (Again) To Become the World's No. 1 Carmaker." *Forbes*, May 22, 2012. http://www.forbes.com/sites/michelinemaynard/2012/05/22/toyota-pushes-past-gm-again-to-become-the-worlds-no-1-carmaker/
6. "Abe Seeks Talks on Boosting Japan's Farm Product Exports." *Jiji Press English News Service*, January 7, 2013.

Chapter 6: A Year Filled with Celebrations

1. Karen Barnaby, "Bean-Eating Said to Bring Good Fortune." *The Vancouver Sun*, January 11, 2006.
2. KCP International Japanese Language School, Sunny Days Ahead with Teru-Teru Bozu. http://www.kcpwindowonjapan.com/2012/12/teru-teru-bozu/

Chapter 7: Language and Learning

1. Naoko Mori, "Languages for the 21st Century." *The Guardian*, February 6, 2010.
2. University of Michigan, Educational Systems of Japan and the US. http://sitemaker.umich.edu/arun.356/structural_differences
3. Japan-101, Takao Doi. http://www.japan-101.com/culture/takao_doi.htm

Chapter 8: Sports and Leisure Time

1. BaseballReference.com, Akinori Iwamura. http://www.baseball-reference.com/bullpen/Akinori_Iwamura
2. Biography.com, Ichiro Suzuki. http://www.biography.com/people/ichiro-suzuki-37219
3. Jeff Passan, "In Ichiro's long road to 4,000, 'every hit is a gift,' not just the milestones." Yahoo! Sports, August 15, 2013. http://sports.yahoo.com/news/in-ichiro%E2%80%99s-long-road-to-4-000--%E2%80%98every-hit-is-a-gift-%E2%80%99-not-just-the-milestones-200549071.html
4. "Ozeki Kaio calls end to illustrious but injury-plagued career." CiberSumo.com, July 9, 2011. http://www.cibersumo.com/index.php/en/press-room-news/111-ozeki-kaio-calls-end-to-illustrious-but-injury-plagued-career
5. Harumi Hotta, "The Exclusive Interview with Ozeki Kaio." *La Monde du Sumo*, April 2006.
6. "Ozeki Kaio calls end…" CiberSumo.com
7. Ibid.

FURTHER READING

Books

Dean, Arlan. *Samurai: Warriors of Japan*. Danbury, Conn.: Children's Press, 2005.

Garcia, Hector. *A Geek in Japan: Discovering the Land of Manga, Anime, Zen, and the Tea Ceremony*. Rutland, Vermont: Tuttle Publishing, 2010.

Mansfield, Stephen. *Japanese Stone Gardens*. North Clarendon, Vermont: Tuttle Publishing, 2009.

Mattern, Joanne. *Ninjas: Masters of Stealth and Secrecy*. Danbury, Conn.: Children's Press, 2005.

WORKS CONSULTED

"Ozeki Kaio calls end to illustrious but injury-plagued career." CiberSumo.com, July 9, 2011. http://www.cibersumo.com/index.php/en/press-room-news/111-ozeki-kaio-calls-end-to-illustrious-but-injury-plagued-career

Japan Reference. http://www.jref.com/

Passan, Jeff. "In Ichiro's long road to 4,000, 'every hit is a gift,' not just the milestones." Yahoo! Sports, August 15, 2013. http://sports.yahoo.com/news/in-ichiro%E2%80%99s-long-road-to-4-000--%E2%80%98every-hit-is-a-gift-%E2%80%99-not-just-the-milestones-200549071.html

Rieber, Beth. *Frommer's Japan*. Hoboken, New Jersey: Wiley Publishing, Inc., 2010.

Rowthorn, Chris et al. *Discover Japan*. Oakland, California: Lonely Planet, 2010.

Soble, Jonathan. "China and Economy to Dominate Abe–US Talks." *FT.com*, February 21, 2013.

Shoenburger, Chana R. "Japan's 10 Most Popular Tourist Attractions." *Forbes*, July 3, 2008.

Woods, Shelton. *Japan: An Illustrated History*. New York: Hippocrene Books, 2004.

Yoder, Stephanie. "Eight Amazing Cultural Experiences in Japan." *Huffington Post*, April 2, 2012. http://travelblog.viator.com/cultural-experiences-japan/

archaeologists (ahr-kee-AWL-uh-jists)—People who study prehistoric people and their cultures through artifacts.

archipelago (ahr-kuh-PEHL-uh-goh)—A large group or chain of islands.

carp (KAHRP)—A large freshwater fish.

curriculum (kuh-RIK-yoo-luhm)—The regular course of study in a school.

conservative (kuhn-SUHR-vuh-tiv)—Traditional in style or manner.

economics (eh-kuh-NAHM-iks)—The science that deals with the production, distribution, consumption, and financial effects of goods and services.

fluent (FLOO-uhnt)—Spoken or written with ease.

hamlet (HAM-luht)—A small village.

hybrid (HIE-brihd)—An automobile that can run either on an electric motor or internal combustion engine.

karma (KAHR-muh)—The cosmic principle that a person is rewarded or punished in this life based on his or her actions in a previous life.

nonferrous (nahn-FEHR-uhs)—Containing little or no iron.

ratify (RAT-uh-fie)—To confirm by expressing formal approval.

reincarnation (ree-in-kahr-NAY-shuhn)—The belief that the soul, upon the death of the body, comes back to earth in another body or form.

sanction (SANGK-shuhn)—A penalty for disobeying a law or rule.

transience (TRAN-zee-uhns)—The quality of lasting only a short time.

trailblazer (TREYL-bley-zer)—A person who forges a path for others to follow in any field or endeavor.

INDEX

Tammy Gagne is the author of numerous books for both adults and children, including *The Nile River* and *We Visit South Africa* for Mitchell Lane Publishers. One of her favorite pastimes is visiting schools to speak to children about the writing process. She resides in northern New England with her husband, son, and a menagerie of animals.